Woman'sDay

Weekend is for Family Meals

The Eat-Well Cookbook of Meals in a Hurry

Woman's Day

Weekend is for Family Meals

The Eat-Well Cookbook of Meals in a Hurry

filipacchi publishing

Contents

✳

SUNDAY DINNERS • 44

Tostados

CHICKEN THIGHS • OVEN • SERVES 4 • ACTIVE: 8 MIN • TOTAL: 15 MIN

8 corn tortillas

Nonstick cooking spray

1 lb boneless, skinless chicken thighs

1½ tsp ground cumin

2 tsp oil

1 firm-ripe avocado

2 Tbsp lime juice

1 can (15.5 oz) black beans, rinsed

¼ cup chopped cilantro

½ cup smooth chipotle salsa

3 to 4 cups chopped romaine lettuce

1. Heat oven to 450°F. Coat corn tortillas with nonstick spray. Place directly on oven rack; bake 8 minutes to crisp.

2. Meanwhile, cut chicken into 1-in. pieces; toss with 1 tsp cumin. Heat oil in large nonstick skillet over medium-high heat. Cook chicken 5 minutes, or until browned and cooked through.

3. Cut avocado into chunks. Toss with lime juice, black beans, cilantro and remaining ½ tsp cumin.

4. Stir salsa into chicken; remove from heat. Serve corn tortillas topped with lettuce, bean mixture and chicken. Serve with additional salsa.

PER SERVING: **468 cal, 34 g pro, 50 g car, 15 g fiber, 16 g fat (3 g sat fat), 94 mg chol, 509 mg sod**

Tropical Chicken Salad

COOKED CHICKEN LEGS AND THIGHS • SALAD • SERVES 4 •
ACTIVE: 15 MIN • TOTAL: 15 MIN

¼ cup light oil & vinegar dressing

2 Tbsp orange juice

1 Tbsp lime zest

¼ tsp pepper

4 grilled chicken legs and
4 thighs, cut in bite-size pieces
(about 4 cups)

1 can (15.5 oz) low-sodium black
beans, rinsed

1 medium red bell pepper,
cut in strips

1 firm-ripe mango, peeled and
cut into bite-size pieces

½ small red onion, sliced

1 head Boston lettuce, torn in pieces

1. Whisk dressing, orange juice, lime zest and pepper in large bowl. Add chicken, beans, pepper strips, mango and onion; toss until evenly coated.

2. Divide lettuce among 4 plates; evenly top with the chicken salad.

PER SERVING: 388 cal, 37 g pro, 35 g car, 8 g fiber,
11 g fat (3 g sat fat), 99 mg chol, 355 mg sod

PER SERVING: 340 cal, 37 g pro,
28 g car, 8 g fiber, 8 g fat (1 g sat fat),
136 mg chol, 632 mg sod

Mustard Chicken on Greens

CHICKEN BREASTS • SKILLET • SERVES 4 • ACTIVE: 10 MIN • TOTAL: 15 MIN

½ cup all-purpose flour

4 boneless, skinless chicken breasts

3 tsp olive oil

1 pint grape tomatoes

½ tsp minced garlic

¾ cup chicken broth

3 Tbsp each grainy Dijon mustard and reduced-fat sour cream

1 Tbsp snipped chives

1 bunch watercress

1. Put flour in large plastic bag, add chicken and shake to coat.

2. Heat 1 tsp of the oil in large nonstick skillet over medium-high heat. Sauté grape tomatoes about 3 minutes or until some begin to soften. Add garlic; cook 30 seconds. Remove to plate.

3. Heat remaining 2 tsp oil in same skillet. Cook chicken about 5 minutes each side, or until instant-read thermometer inserted from side to middle registers 160°F. Remove to plate; cover.

4. Add broth to skillet, stirring to dissolve browned bits. Whisk in mustard and sour cream. Simmer until slightly thickened; add chives.

5. Place chicken on watercress; spoon mustard sauce on top. Serve with tomatoes.

PER SERVING: **215 cal, 29 g pro, 9 g car, 1 g fiber, 6 g fat (2 g sat fat), 70 mg chol, 451 mg sod**

Thai Noodle Bowl

CHICKEN TENDERS · SKILLET · SERVES 4 · ACTIVE: 10 MIN · TOTAL: 15 MIN

4 scallions

½ red bell pepper

1 lb chicken tenders

1 can (14 oz) light coconut milk

½ cup water

1 Tbsp each green curry paste and fish sauce (see Note)

½ a 16-oz box rice noodles

2 tsp oil

2 cups shredded carrots

⅓ cup mint leaves

SERVE WITH: lime wedges

1. Bring 4 cups water to a boil in a 12-in. deep-sided skillet. Meanwhile, slice scallions and red pepper. Cut each chicken tender crosswise in thirds.

2. Whisk coconut milk, ½ cup water, curry paste and fish sauce in bowl until blended.

3. Add noodles to boiling water; cook as package directs.

4. Meanwhile, heat oil in a large nonstick skillet over medium-high heat. Sauté chicken, red pepper and carrots 5 minutes or until cooked through. Add coconut milk mixture; simmer 2 minutes and remove from heat.

5. Add scallions and mint leaves. Drain noodles. Spoon some noodles into each bowl; ladle chicken mixture with broth on top. Serve with lime wedges.

PER SERVING: 483 cal, 30 g pro, 58 g car, 4 g fiber, 13 g fat (6 g sat fat), 66 mg chol, 594 mg sod

NOTE: Green curry paste and fish sauce (nam pla) can be found in your supermarket's Asian food section.

Greek Tacos

GROUND CHICKEN • SKILLET • SERVES 4 • ACTIVE: 10 MIN • TOTAL: 15 MIN

1 lb lean ground chicken

1½ tsp each oregano, paprika and finely minced garlic

½ tsp salt

4 pitas, split, warmed in microwave

2 cups shredded romaine lettuce

1 cup each diced tomatoes and cucumbers

¾ cup plain lowfat yogurt

½ cup crumbled feta cheese

1. Coat large nonstick skillet with cooking spray. Heat over medium-high heat. Add ground chicken, oregano, paprika, garlic and salt.

2. Cook, breaking up chunks with a wooden spoon, until cooked through, about 4 minutes.

3. Top each split pita half with ¼ cup of the lettuce. Add ¼ cup of the chicken mixture, 2 Tbsp each of the tomato and cucumber, 1½ Tbsp of the yogurt and 1 Tbsp of the feta. Fold in half to eat.

PER SERVING: **399 cal, 35 g pro, 44 g car, 7 g fiber, 10 g fat (4 g sat fat), 82 mg chol, 933 mg sod**

Sweet & Crispy Chicken Salad

COOKED CHICKEN NUGGETS · SKILLET · SERVES 4 · ACTIVE: 8 MIN · TOTAL: 13 MIN

1 pkg (12 oz) refrigerated fully-cooked chicken nuggets

⅓ cup orange juice

2 Tbsp red wine vinegar

1½ Tbsp olive oil

½ tsp each salt and pepper

8 cups salad greens (about 6 oz)

2 oranges, peel and white pith removed, halved, sliced

2 cups fresh pineapple chunks

½ cup thinly sliced red onion

GARNISH: cashews

1. Coat a large nonstick skillet with cooking spray; heat over medium-high heat. Add chicken nuggets and cook 4 minutes, turning once, or until browned and heated through.

2. Stir orange juice, vinegar, oil, salt and pepper in large bowl. Add greens, oranges, pineapple and onion; toss to mix and coat.

3. Put salad on serving plates and top with nuggets. Sprinkle with cashews.

PER SERVING: 409 cal, 12 g pro, 37 g car, 4 g fiber, 24 g fat (6 g sat fat), 38 mg chol, 778 mg sod

Chicken Milanese

CHICKEN CUTLETS · SKILLET · SERVES 4 · ACTIVE: 10 MIN · TOTAL: 15 MIN

1 large egg, beaten

1 cup Progresso Panko Crispy Bread Crumbs, Italian Style

1 Tbsp grated Parmesan

4 chicken cutlets

3 Tbsp olive oil

2 Tbsp lemon juice

¼ tsp each salt and pepper

4 cups salad greens

1 can (15 oz) cannellini beans, rinsed

1 cup halved grape tomatoes

½ cup sliced onion

SERVE WITH: lemon wedges

1. Put egg in a shallow bowl. Mix crumbs and cheese on wax paper. Dip cutlets into egg, then into crumbs to coat.

2. Heat 1 Tbsp of the oil in a large nonstick skillet. Add cutlets and cook 5 minutes, turning once, until golden and cooked through. Remove.

3. Whisk remaining 2 Tbsp olive oil, the lemon juice, salt and pepper in a medium bowl. Add remaining ingredients and toss to mix and coat.

4. Serve cutlets topped with salad mixture. Serve with lemon wedges.

PER SERVING: **418 cal, 26 g pro, 39 g car, 5 g fiber, 17 g fat (3 g sat fat), 101 mg chol, 592 mg sod**

Moroccan Chicken & Couscous

CHICKEN THIGHS • SKILLET • SERVES 5 • ACTIVE: 5 MIN • TOTAL: 30 MIN

2 tsp olive oil

4 boneless, skinless chicken thighs, each cut into 3 pieces

¼ tsp salt

1 can (14.5 oz) chicken broth

1 can (14.5 oz) diced tomatoes with garlic and onion

1 pkg (about 1 lb) cubed fresh butternut squash

½ cup raisins

2 tsp ground cumin

1 tsp each ground cinnamon and smoked paprika

1 cup plain couscous

1 cup frozen peas

1. Heat oil in a large deep skillet over medium-high heat. Sprinkle chicken with salt and cook 5 minutes, turning once, until browned. Add broth, tomatoes, squash, raisins, cumin, cinnamon and paprika. Bring to a boil; cover and reduce heat. Simmer 15 minutes or until chicken is tender.

2. Stir in couscous and peas and bring to a boil. Cover, remove skillet from heat and let stand 5 minutes.

PER SERVING: **347 cal, 20 g pro, 58 g car, 7 g fiber, 5 g fat (1 g sat fat), 45 mg chol, 752 mg sod**

Warm Bean & Sausage Salad

TURKEY SAUSAGE • SKILLET • SERVES 4 • ACTIVE: 10 MIN • TOTAL: 25 MIN

※

¾ lb hot or sweet Italian turkey sausage links

½ cup water

⅓ cup reduced-fat vinaigrette

1 Tbsp Dijon mustard

1 medium red onion, sliced

1 jar (8 oz) roasted red peppers, rinsed and sliced

2 cans (15 oz each) cannellini beans, rinsed

⅓ cup pitted Kalamata olives, halved

1 bag (5 oz) baby spinach

1. Spray a large nonstick skillet with cooking spray. Cook sausages over medium-high heat 3 minutes or until browned on one side. Turn sausages over, add water and reduce heat to medium. Cover and cook 5 to 7 minutes until sausage is cooked through. Remove to a plate.

2. While sausage cooks, whisk together vinaigrette and mustard.

3. Add onion to skillet; cover and cook 3 minutes or until softened. Stir in red peppers, beans, olives and vinaigrette mixture. Heat 2 minutes.

4. Slice sausages. Divide spinach among 4 plates; spoon bean mixture and then sausages on top.

PER SERVING: **384 cal, 24 g pro, 44 g car, 11 g fiber, 14 g fat (4 g sat fat), 51 mg chol, 1,545 mg sod**

Turkey Taco Cups

GROUND TURKEY • OVEN • SERVES 4 • ACTIVE: 10 MIN • TOTAL: 25 MIN

Four 10-in. (burrito-size) flour tortillas

Nonstick cooking spray

1 lb ground turkey

1 carrot, shredded

1 package (1 oz) taco seasoning mix

1 cup chopped lettuce

½ cup shredded Cheddar

2 plum tomatoes, seeded and chopped

1. Heat oven to 375°F. Cut three 4¼-in. circles out of each tortilla. Lightly coat tortilla circles with nonstick spray. Place each circle into a muffin pan to shape into a cup. Bake 8 to 9 minutes until crisp. Cool.

2. Meanwhile, cook turkey and carrot with taco seasoning according to package directions. Divide turkey mixture, lettuce, Cheddar and tomatoes among taco cups.

PER SERVING (3 TACOS): 401 cal, 27 g pro, 30 g car, 2 g fiber, 18 g fat (6 g sat fat), 104 mg chol, 996 mg sod

NOTE: No time to make taco cups? Just use taco shells (find them in the ethnic aisle of your grocery store).

Pork with Pineapple BBQ Salsa & Sweet Potatoes

PORK TENDERLOIN • OVEN • SERVES 4 • ACTIVE: 7 MIN • TOTAL: 32 MIN

1 pork tenderloin (about 12 oz)

2 large sweet potatoes, cut in ½-in. wedges

⅓ cup barbecue sauce

¼ cup chopped cilantro

2 tsp oil

½ tsp chili powder

1¼ cups diced fresh or canned pineapple

3 Tbsp chopped red onion

1. Heat oven to 500°F. Position racks to divide oven in thirds. Line 2 rimmed baking sheets with nonstick foil.

2. Place pork on 1 baking sheet, sweet potatoes on the other. Mix 3 Tbsp of the barbecue sauce with 1 Tbsp of the cilantro; brush on pork. Drizzle potatoes with oil; sprinkle with chili powder. Toss to coat; spread evenly.

3. Roast pans 10 minutes; remove from oven. Gently toss sweet potatoes and turn pork. Return to oven; roast potatoes 8 minutes or until tender, pork 15 minutes or until medium.

4. Remove pork to cutting board; let rest while combining pineapple, onion, and remaining cilantro and barbecue sauce in a bowl. Slice pork; top with the pineapple salsa. Serve with sweet potatoes.

PER SERVING: **258 cal, 19 g pro, 33 g car, 4 g fiber, 6 g fat (1 g sat fat), 47 mg chol, 301 mg sod**

Pulled Pork Sandwiches

PORK TENDERLOIN • SKILLET • SERVES 4 (MAKES 8) • ACTIVE: 10 MIN • TOTAL: 15 MIN

1 cup each bottled barbecue sauce and applesauce

1 Tbsp each Worcestershire sauce and brown sugar

2 tsp oil

1 lb pork tenderloin, cut in ¼-in. strips

2 cups coleslaw

8 reduced-calorie hot dog rolls

1. Stir barbecue sauce, applesauce, Worcestershire sauce and brown sugar in a medium bowl until blended.

2. Heat oil in nonstick skillet over medium-high heat. Add pork; cook 2 minutes. Add barbecue sauce mixture, reduce heat and simmer 3 minutes.

3. Spoon coleslaw, then pork, into each bun. Drizzle with any extra sauce.

PER SERVING: 527 cal, 33 g pro, 82 g car, 8 g fiber, 9 g fat (2 g sat fat), 77 mg chol, 1,447 mg sod

Sausage Arugula Pizza

ITALIAN SAUSAGE • SKILLET & OVEN • SERVES 4 • ACTIVE: 5 MIN • TOTAL: 15 MIN

8 oz bulk sweet or hot Italian sausage

½ small red onion, thinly sliced

4 cups baby arugula (about 3 oz)

½ cup roasted red pepper strips

1 large prebaked thin pizza crust (we used Boboli)

¾ cup part-skim ricotta

1 Tbsp grated Parmesan

1. Heat oven to 450°F. Brown sausage in a nonstick skillet over medium-high heat for 5 minutes. Drain off any fat.

2. Add red onion and arugula, sauté 2 minutes until arugula is wilted, then stir in roasted red pepper strips. Spread crust with ½ cup of the ricotta; top with sausage mixture.

3. Dollop with remaining ricotta; sprinkle with Parmesan. Bake directly on oven rack 8 minutes.

PER SERVING: **394 cal, 20 g pro, 41 g car, 2 g fiber, 16 g fat (7 g sat fat), 32 mg chol, 912 mg sod**

Pork Tacos

COOKED PORK LOIN • MICROWAVE • SERVES 4 • ACTIVE: 10 MIN • TOTAL: 15 MIN

❄

1 cup salsa verde (green salsa)

1 cup chopped cilantro

3 cups thick shreds cooked pork loin (see page 58)

8 corn tortillas (heated according to package directions)

1 cup finely shredded lettuce

1 cup diced tomato

1. Mix salsa and cilantro in a microwave-safe bowl. Add pork; toss. Cover and microwave until hot.

2. To make tacos, fill warmed tortillas with pork mixture, then add lettuce and tomato.

PER SERVING: **356 cal, 33 g pro, 30 g car, 4 g fiber, 11 g fat (4 g sat fat), 84 mg chol, 362 mg sod**

TIP: Avocado wedges with a squeeze of lime are a delicious, easy accompaniment.

Moroccan Lamb

LEG OF LAMB • OVEN • SERVES 6 • ACTIVE: 10 MIN • TOTAL: 30 MIN

1 butternut squash (about 2½ lb), peeled, seeded and cut in chunks

2 red peppers, cut in chunks

1 medium onion, cut in chunks

2 tsp minced garlic

1 Tbsp tandoori or garam masala spice blend

½ tsp salt

2 Tbsp olive oil

1¾ lb boneless leg of lamb, cut in 1-in. pieces

1 Tbsp chopped cilantro

1. Heat oven to 500°F. Position racks to divide oven in thirds. Line 2 rimmed baking sheets with nonstick foil.

2. Mix squash, peppers and onion in a large bowl. Combine garlic, spice blend, salt and oil in a small bowl. Add 1 Tbsp to vegetables; toss to coat. Spread evenly on 1 baking sheet.

3. Place on high oven rack; roast 10 minutes.

4. Meanwhile, put lamb in large bowl. Add remaining spice mixture; toss to coat. Spread on other baking sheet. Move vegetables to low rack; put meat on high rack.

5. Roast 10 minutes, or until lamb is cooked through and vegetables are tender. Gently toss meat with the vegetables; sprinkle with cilantro.

PER SERVING: 300 cal, 28 g pro, 25 g car, 5 g fiber, 11 g fat (3 g sat fat), 78 mg chol, 263 mg sod

Chimichurri Steak

SKIRT STEAK • GRILL • SERVES 4 • ACTIVE: 8 MIN • TOTAL: 18 MIN

1½ lb sweet potatoes, peeled and cut into ¾-in. pieces

2 Tbsp light oil & vinegar dressing

1 Tbsp Dijon mustard

2 scallions, chopped

1 lb skirt steak, cut in 4 equal pieces

½ tsp each paprika and salt

1 clove garlic

½ bunch cilantro (about 1 cup packed cilantro)

3 Tbsp olive oil

2 Tbsp lime juice

½ tsp crushed hot pepper flakes

1. Steam potatoes 10 minutes or until tender; rinse under cold water and toss with dressing, mustard and scallions. Chill or serve at room temperature.

2. Heat grill or stovetop grill pan. Rub steaks with paprika and salt. Grill 2 to 3 minutes on each side for medium-rare. Remove to plate; let stand.

3. Pulse garlic and cilantro in food processor until finely chopped. Remove to bowl; stir in olive oil, lime juice and hot pepper flakes. Spoon onto steak.

PER SERVING: **400 cal, 24 g pro, 27 g car, 4 g fiber, 22 g fat (6 g sat fat), 51 mg chol, 566 mg sod**

Best Burger

1 lb ground sirloin

¼ lb ground chuck

1½ tsp Worcestershire sauce

¼ tsp each kosher (coarse) salt and pepper

Nonstick cooking spray

SERVE WITH: hamburger buns, lettuce, tomato and red onion slices

1. Heat outdoor grill or grill pan.

2. Gently mix ground meats and Worcestershire sauce in medium bowl with a fork until blended. Shape meat into four patties about 1 in. thick. Sprinkle both sides of patties with salt and pepper.

3. Coat burgers with nonstick spray. Grill, turning once, 8 to 10 minutes, until instant-read thermometer inserted from side to middle registers 160°F. Serve on buns with lettuce, sliced tomato and red onion.

PER SERVING (BURGER ONLY): **239 cal, 30 g pro, 0 g car, 0 g fiber, 12 g fat (5 g sat fat), 72 mg chol, 209 mg sod**

TIP: Blending ground sirloin and chuck creates the perfect burger. Sirloin gives delicious flavor and chuck ensures juiciness.

Sweet & Sour Shrimp and Ginger-Soy Beef

✳

GETTING STARTED

Make a sauce, *right,* then go to page 30 to pick protein, veggies, sides and finishing touches. Follow these cooking steps:

1. Heat 1 Tbsp oil in large nonstick skillet. Put 2 Tbsp cornstarch and 1 lb protein into a large ziptop bag, seal bag and shake to coat.

2. Add protein to skillet; stir-fry over medium-high heat 3 to 5 minutes or until cooked through. Remove to plate.

3. Add 2 tsp oil to skillet; heat. Add 4 cups of any one or combination of vegetables; stir-fry 3 to 5 minutes or until crisp-tender.

4. Add sauce to skillet; bring to simmer. Add protein; simmer 1 to 2 minutes until sauce thickens and coats mixture.

5. Serve with choice of side, and top with finishing touches.

4 Sauces That Give You a World of Flavor

THAI-COCONUT
Whisk a 14-oz can light coconut milk, 2 Tbsp brown sugar, 1 Tbsp green curry paste, ¼ cup chopped cilantro or mint and ¼ tsp salt in small bowl until blended.

SWEET & SOUR
Stir ½ cup apricot preserves, ¼ cup ketchup, 2 Tbsp cider vinegar and 1 tsp minced garlic in small bowl until blended.

PEANUT
Whisk 1 cup water, ⅓ cup creamy peanut butter, 2 Tbsp reduced-sodium soy sauce, 2 tsp minced garlic and ¼ tsp crushed red pepper in small bowl until blended.

GINGER-SOY
Stir ½ cup orange juice, ¼ cup reduced-sodium soy sauce, 2 Tbsp honey, 2 Tbsp water, 1 Tbsp grated ginger, 1 Tbsp minced scallion, 2 tsp cornstarch and 1 tsp sesame oil in small bowl until cornstarch is dissolved.

PROTEIN (1 LB)

- shelled shrimp
- boneless, skinless chicken breasts, cut in ¾-in. cubes
- boneless sirloin, flank or skirt steak, cut into ¼-in.-thick strips
- pork tenderloin, cut lengthwise in half, then crosswise into ¼-in. slices
- firm tofu, cut into 1-in. cubes

VEGETABLES (4 CUPS)

- small broccoli florets
- small cauliflower florets
- sliced shiitake mushrooms
- sliced white button mushrooms
- shelled edamame
- ½-in. red or yellow pepper strips
- ½-in. cubanelle pepper strips
- thinly sliced carrots
- 1½-in.-long slices asparagus
- snow peas
- ½-in.-thick red onion wedges

SIDES

- jasmine rice
- brown rice
- buckwheat noodles
- cellophane/rice noodles
- lo mein noodles or stir-fry noodles

FINISHING TOUCHES

- cashews, peanuts or almonds
- toasted sesame seeds
- crushed red pepper
- thinly sliced scallions
- cilantro
- mint

OPPOSITE: Ginger-Soy Beef.

Mediterranean Tuna

CANNED TUNA • SALAD • SERVES 4 • ACTIVE: 5 MIN • TOTAL: 13 MIN

8 oz green beans, ends trimmed

2 bags (8 oz each) Mediterranean salad greens, or other lettuce greens

2 cucumbers, peeled, halved, seeded and sliced

1 pt grape tomatoes

1 can (12 oz) chunk light tuna in oil, drained

12 country-style mixed Kalamata olives

¼ cup each Greek salad dressing and crumbled basil-and-tomato feta cheese

1. Cook green beans in water to cover, or steam 7 to 8 minutes just until crisp-tender. Drain well.

2. Empty the salad greens into a large bowl. Toss together with vegetables, tuna, olives, dressing and cheese.

PER SERVING: **385 cal, 25 g pro, 40 g car, 6 g fiber, 25 g fat (5 g sat fat), 50 mg chol, 1,016 mg sod**

Mediterranean Shrimp & Bulgur

SHRIMP • SALAD • SERVES 4 • ACTIVE: 15 MIN • TOTAL: 20 MIN

¾ cup bulgur (cracked wheat)

½ large seedless cucumber

3 scallions

½ cup mint leaves

1 lb frozen cooked large shrimp, thawed

1 pint grape tomatoes

¼ cup lemon juice

2 Tbsp olive oil

¼ tsp each salt and pepper

3 cups baby arugula

2 oz feta cheese, crumbled

1. Put bulgur in large bowl. Add boiling water to cover; let soak 15 minutes.

2. Meanwhile, coarsely chop cucumber, scallions and mint leaves.

3. Drain bulgur well, return to bowl and add shrimp, tomatoes, cucumber, scallions, mint, lemon juice, olive oil, salt and pepper. Toss with arugula. Sprinkle with feta.

PER SERVING: **336 cal, 31 g pro,
29 g car, 8 g fiber, 12 g fat (3 g sat fat),
234 mg chol, 574 mg sod**

Asian Tilapia Salad

TILAPIA FILLETS • OVEN • SERVES 4 • ACTIVE: 10 MIN • TOTAL: 17 MIN

1 lb tilapia, cut into 1½-in.-thick strips

3 scallions, chopped

¼ cup sesame ginger dressing, divided

1 can (15 oz) sliced baby corn, drained and rinsed

1 bag (10 oz) mixed salad greens

1. In a medium bowl, combine tilapia and scallions with 2 Tbsp of the sesame ginger dressing. Refrigerate 10 minutes.

2. Heat broiler. Place tilapia on a foil-lined baking sheet and broil for 7 minutes or until fish is cooked through.

3. Toss remaining 2 Tbsp dressing with baby corn and salad greens until lightly coated. Divide salad and fish among plates.

PER SERVING: **230 cal**, 30 g pro, 12 g car, 7 g fiber, 7 g fat (1 g sat fat), 57 mg chol, 479 mg sod

Shrimp & Sugar Snap Sauté

SHRIMP • SKILLET • SERVES 4 • ACTIVE: 5 MIN • TOTAL: 10 MIN

❋

1 Tbsp butter

1½ lb frozen extra-large peeled and deveined shrimp, thawed

1 pkg (8 oz) trimmed sugar snap peas

¼ tsp each salt and pepper

1 pt grape tomatoes

1 tsp minced garlic

3 Tbsp chopped parsley

1½ tsp lemon zest

SERVE WITH: bread and lemon wedges (optional)

1. Melt butter in a large nonstick skillet. Add shrimp, peas, salt and pepper. Cook over medium-high heat 3 minutes, stirring often.

2. Add tomatoes and garlic to skillet, cover and, shaking pan often, cook 2 minutes or until tomatoes soften and shrimp are cooked through. Stir in parsley and lemon zest. Serve with bread and lemon wedges.

PER SERVING: **251 cal, 37 g pro, 10 g car, 2 g fiber, 6 g fat (2 g sat fat), 266 mg chol, 429 mg sod**

Greek-Style Shrimp & Cannellini Beans

SHRIMP • OVEN • SERVES 4 • ACTIVE: 10 MIN • TOTAL: 30 MIN

1 lb (16 to 20 per lb) peeled and deveined shrimp

1 can (about 15 oz) cannellini beans, rinsed and drained

1 pint cherry tomatoes, halved

6 oz fresh green beans, halved

¼ cup Kalamata olives, sliced

2 Tbsp olive oil

2 tsp grated lemon zest

1 tsp minced garlic

¼ tsp each pepper and dried oregano

GARNISH: crumbled feta cheese, lemon wedges

1. Place oven rack in center of oven. Heat oven to 500°F. You'll need a rimmed baking pan and 4 pieces of nonstick foil (each about 16 in. long).

2. Put all ingredients in a large bowl and toss to mix. Lay the 4 sheets of foil on countertop. Place ¼ of the shrimp mixture in center of each piece.

3. Bring one side of opposite ends together. Double-fold to seal, then seal other sides. Place packets sealed side up on baking pan.

4. Bake 15 minutes. Open one packet to check doneness of shrimp. If shrimp aren't cooked through, reseal packet and bake another 5 minutes or until cooked through.

5. Transfer contents of each packet to serving plates. Sprinkle with feta cheese and serve with lemon wedges.

PER SERVING: **311 cal, 29 g pro, 23 g car, 7 g fiber, 11 g fat (2 g sat fat), 172 mg chol, 460 mg sod**

Cod & Asparagus with Tomato Vinaigrette

COD FILLETS • OVEN • SERVES 5 • ACTIVE: 7 MIN • TOTAL: 20 MIN

2 lb cod fillets (1½ in. thick), cut in five pieces

1 bunch (about 1¼ lb) asparagus, woody ends snapped off

Garlic-flavor nonstick spray

½ tsp each salt and pepper

1 cup diced plum tomatoes

¼ cup olive oil & vinegar dressing

2 Tbsp chopped fresh tarragon, basil, chives, parsley or dill

SERVE WITH: 10 slices (each ¾ in. thick) French bread

1. Heat oven to 500°F. Position racks to divide oven in thirds. Line 2 rimmed baking sheets with nonstick foil.

2. Place fish on 1 baking sheet; spread asparagus evenly on the other. Coat cod and asparagus with nonstick spray; sprinkle with salt and pepper.

3. Roast 10 to 12 minutes, switching position of pans halfway through cooking, until cod is just cooked through and asparagus are tender.

4. Mix remaining ingredients in a bowl. Spoon over cod. Serve with bread.

PER SERVING: 430 cal, 40 g pro, 50 g car, 4 g fiber, 7 g fat (1 g sat fat), 69 mg chol, 1,032 mg sod

Ginger-Soy Salmon & Bok Choy

SALMON FILLETS • SKILLET & OVEN • SERVES 4 • ACTIVE: 10 MIN • TOTAL: 25 MIN

2 tsp canola oil

2 Tbsp minced fresh ginger

2 tsp minced garlic

1½ lb bok choy, halved lengthwise, then sliced crosswise in 1-in. strips

4 oz shiitake mushrooms, stems discarded, caps sliced

1 cup shredded carrots

4 salmon fillets (5 to 6 oz each)

3 Tbsp reduced-sodium soy sauce

3 Tbsp orange marmalade

GARNISH: toasted sesame seeds

SERVE WITH: 90-second microwavable brown rice

1. Heat broiler. Heat oil in a large, deep ovenproof nonstick skillet. Add 1 Tbsp ginger and the garlic; cook over low heat a few seconds until fragrant.

2. Add bok choy, mushrooms and carrots. Stir-fry 4 to 6 minutes, until bok choy and carrots are crisp-tender. Remove to a serving bowl; cover to keep warm.

3. Place salmon skin side down in skillet. In a small cup, mix remaining 1 Tbsp ginger, the soy sauce and marmalade. Spoon about half of soy sauce mixture over salmon.

4. Broil 4 to 6 minutes until salmon is just cooked through. Drizzle with remaining soy sauce mixture and serve with the vegetables. Top with sesame seeds, if desired.

PER SERVING: **363 cal, 38 g pro, 20 g car, 3 g fiber, 14 g fat (2 g sat fat), 99 mg chol, 879 mg sod**

Eggplant-Polenta Stacks

VEGETARIAN • SKILLET • SERVES 4 • ACTIVE: 15 MIN • TOTAL: 30 MIN

※

1 Tbsp plus 2 tsp olive oil

1 small eggplant (8 oz), halved, sliced (3 cups)

¾ cup chopped onion

2 small zucchini (8 oz), sliced (2 cups)

¼ cup sliced sun-dried tomatoes

¼ tsp each salt and pepper

1 tube (16 to 18 oz) ready-to-heat polenta, cut into 8 slices

1 large plum tomato, cut into 8 slices

½ cup shredded part-skim mozzarella

GARNISH: chopped fresh basil

SERVE WITH: 1 cup marinara sauce, heated in microwave

1. Heat 1 Tbsp of the oil in a large, deep nonstick skillet. Add eggplant and onion. Cover and cook over medium-high heat 4 minutes, stirring a few times, until slightly softened.

2. Add 1 tsp of the remaining oil, the zucchini, sun-dried tomatoes, salt and pepper. Cover and cook 6 to 7 minutes, stirring often, until vegetables are tender. Remove to bowl; wipe or rinse skillet.

3. Heat remaining 1 tsp oil in skillet. Add polenta; cook 2 minutes over medium-high heat until bottoms are golden.

4. Off heat, flip polenta and spoon the vegetable mixture onto polenta (it's OK if some falls onto the skillet). Top each with 1 slice of tomato and sprinkle with cheese.

5. Place skillet over low heat; cover and cook 2 minutes or until cheese melts. Sprinkle with basil, if desired, and serve with sauce.

PER SERVING: **282 cal, 9 g pro, 39 g car, 6 g fiber, 10 g fat (3 g sat fat), 9 mg chol, 948 mg sod**

Cuban Beans

VEGETARIAN · SKILLET · SERVES 4 · ACTIVE: 5 MIN · TOTAL: 15 MIN

2 tsp oil

4 cloves garlic, minced

2 cans (15.5 oz each) black beans, rinsed

1 cup water

1½ tsp ground cumin

1 tsp dried oregano

1 tsp smoked or regular paprika

¼ tsp pepper

1 bag (1 lb) frozen pepper stir-fry vegetable blend (sliced green, red and yellow peppers and onions)

SERVE WITH: cooked rice, lime wedges, hot sauce

1. Heat oil in large skillet over medium-high heat. Add garlic; cook 30 seconds.

2. Stir in remaining ingredients. Bring to simmer, cover and reduce heat. Cook 10 minutes or until vegetables are tender and flavors have blended.

PER SERVING: **265 cal, 15 g pro, 45 g car, 17 g fiber, 3 g fat (0 g sat fat), 0 mg chol, 521 mg sod**

Low & Slow Ribs

BABY-BACK RIBS • OVEN & GRILL • SERVES 8 • ACTIVE: 10 MIN • TOTAL: 3 HR

1 Tbsp each seasoned salt and sugar

1½ tsp each salt-free chili powder and onion powder

½ tsp pumpkin pie spice

2 racks baby-back ribs (about 3¾ lb)

½ cup water

½ cup barbecue sauce

1. Heat oven to 300°F. You'll need a large roasting pan and a rack.

2. In a cup, mix seasoned salt, sugar, chili and onion powders, and pumpkin pie spice. Rub all over ribs; place ribs rounded side up on rack in pan.

3. Pour water into bottom of roasting pan; cover with foil and bake 2½ to 3 hours until ribs are very tender.

4. Heat outdoor grill. Brush ribs with half the barbecue sauce. Grill 5 minutes or until lightly charred, turning as needed and brushing with remaining sauce. Cut into individual ribs to serve.

PER SERVING: 324 cal, 19 g pro, 9 g car, 0 g fiber, 23 g fat (9 g sat fat), 100 mg chol, 800 mg sod

TIP: The ribs can be cooked 2 days ahead, then covered and refrigerated. To serve, let ribs sit out on the counter for 10 minutes (while the grill heats), then follow step 4.

Beef Stew Casserole

BEEF CHUCK • OVEN • SERVES 8 • ACTIVE: 45 MIN • TOTAL: 1 HR 35 MIN

1½ lb 1-in. cubes beef chuck (for stew)

¼ cup all-purpose flour

1½ Tbsp vegetable oil

2 cans (about 14 oz each) beef broth

1 large onion, sliced

1 Tbsp minced garlic

3 lb small sweet potatoes

1 lb each carrots and parsnips

3 ribs celery

1 Tbsp butter

¼ tsp salt

1. Position racks to divide oven in thirds. Heat to 325°F.

2. Coat beef with flour. Heat oil in a Dutch oven over medium-high heat. Add beef and brown. Add broth, onion and garlic; bring to a boil. Cover tightly and place stew on one oven rack, potatoes on other rack. Bake 30 minutes.

3. Cut carrots, parsnips and celery into 1-in. lengths; stir into stew. Cover and bake 45 minutes or until tender when pierced.

4. Peel potatoes and mash with butter and salt. Bake and serve or cool, cover separately and refrigerate up to 3 days.

5. To SERVE: Heat oven to 400°F. Skim fat off stew, then spoon into a shallow 3½-qt baking dish; spread potatoes over top. Bake 50 minutes or until bubbly around edges and hot in center.

PER SERVING: **488 cal**, 20 g pro, 53 g car, 9 g fiber, 22 g fat (8 g sat fat), 66 mg chol, 550 mg sod

Curried Beef Samosas

GROUND BEEF • OVEN & SKILLET • SERVES 4 • ACTIVE: 30 MIN • TOTAL: 50 MIN

1 box (15 oz) refrigerated pie crusts

2 tsp oil

1 cup diced potato

½ cup chopped onion

8 oz lean ground beef

2 Tbsp curry powder

1 Tbsp each minced garlic and ginger

¼ tsp each salt and pepper

1 cup frozen petite peas

½ cup chicken broth or water

1 large egg, slightly beaten

SERVE WITH: purchased chutney

1. Heat oven to 400°F. Coat a baking sheet with nonstick spray. Let pie crusts sit at room temperature for about 15 minutes.

2. Meanwhile, heat oil in large nonstick skillet over medium-high heat. Sauté potato and onion 4 minutes or until almost tender. Add beef; cook 2 minutes, breaking up, until no longer pink. Drain off any excess fat. Return to heat.

3. Stir in curry powder, garlic, ginger, salt and pepper; cook 1 minute. Stir in peas and chicken broth; cook 2 minutes until almost dry and potatoes are tender. Remove from heat; let cool slightly.

4. Unroll a pie crust on cutting board. Cut into 4 equal wedges. Moisten edges of 1 wedge with water. Place ⅓ cup filling onto half of wedge, leaving about a ½-in. border on two sides. Fold in half to make a triangle, pressing edges to seal in filling. Transfer to baking sheet. Repeat with remaining crust and filling.

5. Brush lightly with egg. Bake 15 to 20 minutes until golden. Serve samosas warm with chutney on the side.

PER SERVING: **689 cal, 19 g pro, 68 g car, 4 g fiber, 37 g fat (14 g sat fat), 107 mg chol, 726 mg sod**

Greek Cigars

GROUND BEEF · SKILLET & OVEN · MAKES 28 · ACTIVE: 40 MIN · TOTAL: 1 HR

❋

8 oz lean ground beef

½ cup finely chopped onion

1 pkg (10 oz) frozen leaf spinach, thawed, drained and coarsely chopped

½ tsp each salt and ground nutmeg

¼ tsp pepper

3 oz crumbled feta cheese (about ½ cup)

3 Tbsp chopped fresh dill

1 roll fillo (½ a 1-lb box; we used Athens), thawed

½ cup melted butter

1 cup plain yogurt

1. Heat medium skillet over medium-high heat. Add beef and onion; cook 3 minutes, breaking up meat, until no longer pink. Add spinach, ¼ tsp salt, the nutmeg and pepper; cook 2 minutes. Remove from heat; stir in feta and 1 Tbsp dill until well blended.

2. Heat oven to 400°F. Line a 15 x 10-in. baking pan with foil; coat with nonstick cooking spray. Unfold fillo. Lay a sheet, with short side facing you, on work surface; keep remaining sheets covered with plastic wrap topped with a damp towel. Lightly brush top half of fillo sheet with butter. Fold unbuttered half on top of buttered half to make a 6 x 8-in. rectangle and brush again. Cut in half to make two 6 x 4-in. rectangles.

3. Place 1 Tbsp filling along a short side of one rectangle; roll up into a tight cylinder. Place on baking pan, seam side down; brush with butter. Repeat with remaining fillo and filling.

4. Bake 12 minutes or until golden. Meanwhile, stir remaining 2 Tbsp chopped dill and ¼ tsp salt with yogurt in small bowl. Serve cigars warm with yogurt-dill sauce.

PER CIGAR: **86 cal, 3 g pro, 5 g car, 0 g fiber, 6 g fat (3 g sat fat), 18 mg chol, 163 mg sod**

CLOCKWISE FROM LEFT: Greek Cigars, Chipotle-Orange BBQ Meatballs, Steamed Chinese Dumplings

Steamed Chinese Dumplings

GROUND BEEF • SKILLET WITH STEAMER BASKET • MAKES 42 •
ACTIVE: 30 MIN • TOTAL: 1 HR

DUMPLINGS

12 oz lean ground beef

1 can (8 oz) sliced water chestnuts, drained and chopped

⅓ cup sliced scallions

1 Tbsp each minced garlic and ginger

1 Tbsp each lite soy sauce and rice wine vinegar

1 pkg (12 oz) wonton wrappers

DIPPING SAUCE

½ cup each lite soy sauce and rice wine vinegar

2 Tbsp sliced scallions

1 tsp each minced ginger, dark sesame oil and sugar

¼ tsp crushed red pepper flakes

1. DUMPLINGS: Put a steamer basket into a large nonstick skillet. Add just enough water to almost come up to the bottom of the basket. Line a baking sheet with foil or wax paper. Fill a small bowl with water.

2. Combine beef, water chestnuts, scallions, garlic, ginger, soy sauce and vinegar in a bowl. Mix with your hands or a wooden spoon until blended.

3. Put 4 wonton wrappers on work surface. Place 1 heaping tsp beef mixture in center of each. Dip your finger in bowl of water and run it along edges of wrappers. Bring up 1 set of opposite corners of wrapper over filling and pinch to seal. Bring up other set of opposite corners and pinch to seal. Place on prepared baking sheet. Repeat with remaining filling and wrappers.

4. Put as many dumplings as will fit in an even layer in steamer basket. Cover and steam 10 to 12 minutes until dough is tender and center is cooked through (you'll need to cut one open to check). Remove dumplings and repeat with remaining dumplings. (If the first batch cools off before serving, they can be reheated in microwave.)

5. DIPPING SAUCE: Stir all ingredients in a small bowl until blended and sugar dissolves. Serve with dumplings.

PER DUMPLING: 44 cal, 2 g pro, 6 g car, 0 g fiber,
1 g fat (0 g sat fat), 6 mg chol, 245 mg sod

Chipotle-Orange BBQ Meatballs

GROUND BEEF • SKILLET • MAKES 30 • ACTIVE: 15 MIN • TOTAL: 22 MIN

❄

12 oz lean ground beef

½ cup crushed tortilla chips

½ cup chopped cilantro

⅓ cup sliced scallions

1 large egg

1 tsp each cumin, oregano and minced garlic

⅔ cup chipotle or regular barbecue sauce

1½ tsp grated orange zest

¼ cup orange juice

1. Using your hands, mix beef, chips, ⅓ cup of the cilantro, the scallions, egg, cumin, oregano and garlic in a medium bowl until well combined. Form into 30 balls (about 1 Tbsp each).

2. Coat large nonstick skillet with nonstick spray; heat over medium heat. Add meatballs; increase heat to medium-high and cook 5 to 7 minutes, turning frequently, until browned and cooked through.

3. Add barbecue sauce, orange zest and juice, and remaining cilantro to skillet. Cook, tossing, over low heat until meatballs are coated. Transfer to serving bowl and serve with toothpicks.

PER MEATBALL: 43 cal, 3 g pro, 4 g car, 0 g fiber, 2 g fat (1 g sat fat), 14 mg chol, 90 mg sod

Meatball Souvlaki

GROUND BEEF • OVEN • SERVES 4 • ACTIVE: 20 MIN • TOTAL: 45 MIN

YOGURT SAUCE

1 cup plain Greek yogurt

⅓ cup chopped fresh mint

¼ cup water

¼ tsp each ground cumin, garlic powder and salt

MEATBALLS

⅓ cup plain dry bread crumbs

1 large egg

⅓ cup water

1 Tbsp dried minced onion

1 tsp ground cumin

¼ tsp each garlic powder, salt and pepper

1 lb lean ground beef

1 lb medium zucchini, cut into ½-in. rounds

1 medium red onion, cut into ½-in.-thick wedges

2 tsp olive oil

3 plum tomatoes, cut into 4 wedges

SERVE WITH: Warmed pocketless pitas, lettuce (optional)

1. Position racks to divide oven in thirds. Heat oven to 500°F. Line 2 rimmed baking pans with nonstick foil.

2. YOGURT SAUCE: Mix all sauce ingredients in medium bowl, cover and refrigerate until ready to serve with meatballs.

3. MEATBALLS: Stir bread crumbs, egg, water, minced onion, cumin, garlic powder, salt and pepper until blended. Add beef; stir with fork until thoroughly blended. Roll rounded Tbsps into balls; place on a lined baking pan.

4. Put zucchini and red onion on other lined baking pan; toss with oil. Place vegetables on top rack, meatballs on bottom. Roast 20 minutes.

5. Remove pans from oven, turn browned vegetables over, then push to one side and add tomatoes; turn meatballs. Roast meatballs and vegetables 5 minutes more or until zucchini is tender; toss together.

6. Serve on pitas with lettuce if desired. Top with the yogurt sauce.

PER SERVING: **363 cal, 31 g pro, 17 g car, 3 g fiber, 19 g fat (9 g sat fat), 132 mg chol, 450 mg sod**

Italian Orzo & Beef Stuffed Peppers

GROUND BEEF • OVEN & SKILLET • SERVES 4 • ACTIVE: 10 MIN • TOTAL: 35 MIN

4 large bell peppers, halved lengthwise through stem, seeded

Nonstick spray

½ cup orzo pasta

8 oz lean ground beef

1 cup chopped onion

2 tsp each fennel seeds and oregano

1 can (14.5 oz) diced tomatoes with garlic

½ cup diced part-skim mozzarella

GARNISH: chopped basil (optional)

1. Heat broiler. Line a rimmed baking sheet with nonstick foil. Put peppers cut side down in pan; coat peppers with nonstick spray.

2. Broil 12 minutes, turning once, until lightly charred and tender. Reduce oven temperature to 400°F.

3. Meanwhile, bring a medium pot of lightly salted water to a boil. Add orzo and cook as package directs; drain.

4. While pasta cooks, coat a large nonstick skillet with nonstick spray; heat over medium heat. Add beef, onion, fennel seeds and oregano. Cook 6 minutes, breaking up meat with a wooden spoon, until beef is browned and onions are tender. Remove from heat.

5. Add orzo, tomatoes with their juices, and mozzarella to skillet; toss to mix, then fill peppers. Bake 5 minutes or until cheese melts. Sprinkle with basil.

PER SERVING: **328 cal, 22 g pro, 36 g car, 6 g fiber, 11 g fat (5 g sat fat), 46 mg chol, 437 mg sod**

Ham & Mushroom Strata

SMOKED HAM • SKILLET & OVEN • SERVES 8 • ACTIVE: 50 MIN • TOTAL: 1 HR 50 MIN

1 Tbsp stick butter

1 cup finely chopped onion

10 oz mushrooms, sliced

1 piece (8 oz) boneless smoked ham, cubed

1 bag (16 oz) broccoli florets, steamed

8 slices sandwich bread, cubed

6 oz fontina cheese, shredded (1½ cups)

6 large eggs

3 cups whole milk

¼ tsp pepper

1. Lightly coat a shallow 3-qt baking dish with nonstick spray.

2. Melt butter in a large skillet. Add onion; sauté until tender. Add mushrooms; sauté until browned and dry. Stir in ham and broccoli.

3. Spread half the bread cubes in prepared baking dish. Top with ham mixture and half the cheese. Scatter remaining bread over top. Whisk eggs, milk and pepper in a large bowl until blended. Pour evenly over bread; sprinkle with remaining cheese. Bake and serve, or cover and refrigerate up to 1 day.

4. To SERVE: Heat oven to 350°F. Bake uncovered 1 hour or until top is puffed and lightly browned, and a wooden pick inserted in center comes out dry.

PER SERVING: **365 cal, 26 g pro,** 24 g car, 3 g fiber, 19 g fat (9 g sat fat), 221 mg chol, 1,217 mg sod

Ranchero Pork

PORK SHOULDER ROAST • SLOW COOKER • SERVES 8 •
ACTIVE: 18 MIN • TOTAL: 8 TO 10 HR ON LOW

1 can (14 oz) mild red enchilada sauce

1 can (4 oz) diced green chiles

3½ lb bone-in pork shoulder roast, well trimmed

1 medium red onion, sliced

¼ cup fresh lime juice

½ cup chopped fresh cilantro

SERVE WITH: warm corn tortillas

1. Mix enchilada sauce and chiles in a 4-qt or larger slow cooker. Add pork; spoon sauce over top. Cover and cook on low 8 to 10 hours until pork is very tender.

2. At least 20 minutes before serving, toss onion slices with lime juice in a medium bowl. Let stand, tossing once or twice until slightly wilted.

3. Remove pork to a cutting board. Stir cilantro into mixture in slow cooker. Break pork into bite-size chunks with a wooden spoon and return to cooker; stir to combine.

4. To SERVE: Spoon pork mixture on warmed tortillas, top with marinated onions, fold and eat.

PER SERVING: **268 cal, 29 g pro, 9 g car, 1 g fiber, 12 g fat (4 g sat fat), 97 mg chol, 607 mg sod**

Pork with Mole Sauce

PORK LOIN ROAST • SLOW COOKER • SERVES 4 •
ACTIVE: 10 MIN • TOTAL: 5 TO 8 HR ON LOW

1 can (14.5 oz) fire-roasted diced tomatoes

¾ cup sliced onion

¼ cup each raisins and toasted sliced almonds

2 Tbsp each salt-free chili powder and sliced garlic

¼ tsp ground cinnamon

One 2¾-lb boneless pork loin roast, well trimmed

1½ oz bittersweet chocolate, chopped

1. Mix all ingredients except pork and chocolate in a 3-qt or larger slow cooker. Add pork; spoon some of the tomato mixture over pork.

2. Cover and cook on low 5 to 8 hours until pork is fork-tender. Remove pork to cutting board. Add chocolate to slow cooker; stir until melted.

3. Transfer about half of the sauce in slow cooker to a food processor; process until smooth. Stir into remaining sauce in slow cooker.

4. Cut pork roast in half; wrap and save one half for Pork Tacos recipe (see page 23). Slice remaining pork. Serve topped with sauce.

PER SERVING: **409 cal, 42 g pro, 25 g car, 4 g fiber, 16 g fat (5 g sat fat), 107 mg chol, 315 mg sod**

Mexican Pork & Sweet Potato Stew

PORK TENDERLOIN • SKILLET • SERVES 6 • ACTIVE: 10 MIN • TOTAL: 30 MIN

❋

1 Tbsp olive oil

1¼ lb pork tenderloin, cut bite-size

1½ lb sweet potatoes, peeled and cubed

2 poblano chile peppers, seeded and sliced

1 cup chopped onion

1 Tbsp chopped garlic

½ tsp ground cumin

¼ tsp ground cinnamon

1 can (14 oz) reduced-sodium chicken broth

½ cup water

1 cup frozen corn kernels

1½ cups salsa

GARNISH: chopped cilantro, tortilla strips (optional)

1. Heat 2 tsp of the oil in a deep nonstick skillet. Add pork; cook over medium-high heat 7 minutes or until browned. Transfer pork to a plate.

2. Heat remaining 1 tsp oil in skillet. Add potatoes, peppers and onion. Cover; cook 5 minutes, stirring, until peppers and onion soften slightly.

3. Stir in garlic, cumin and cinnamon; cook a few seconds until fragrant. Add broth and water; bring to a boil. Add corn; cover and cook 5 minutes or until vegetables soften.

4. Stir in salsa and pork; heat through. Sprinkle servings with cilantro and tortilla strips if desired.

PER SERVING: **268 cal, 23 g pro, 31 g car, 4 g fiber, 5 g fat (1 g sat fat), 61 mg chol, 474 mg sod**

Bacon-Wrapped Pork Tenderloin

PORK TENDERLOIN • OVEN • SERVES 5 • ACTIVE: 10 MIN • TOTAL: 40 MIN

❋

1 pork tenderloin (about 1¼ lb)

3 scallions, trimmed and cut lengthwise in strips

5 strips lower-sodium bacon

½ tsp pepper

1 Tbsp sugar

1. Heat oven to 425°F. Make a long slit lengthwise down center of pork, being careful not to cut all the way through. Open like a book. Place scallions on one cut side of pork; fold pork back over to close.

2. Wrap bacon slices around pork to cover completely. Place in small roasting pan. Rub pepper and sugar over bacon. Roast 20 minutes or until instant-read thermometer inserted in center reads 150°F. Let stand 10 minutes before slicing.

PER SERVING: 172 cal, 25 g pro, 4 g car, 0 g fiber, 6 g fat (2 g sat fat), 69 mg chol, 134 mg sod

DIFFERENT TAKES
- Spread pork with Dijon mustard before wrapping with bacon.
- Rub bacon with brown sugar instead of granulated sugar.
- Substitute fresh chopped herbs for the scallions.

Pork Lo Mein

PORK CUTLETS • SKILLET • SERVES 4 • ACTIVE: 10 MIN • TOTAL: 25 MIN

❄

2 packages (3 oz each)
Oriental-flavor ramen noodle soup

2 tsp oil

1 large onion, sliced

3 cloves garlic, minced

1 bag (1 lb) frozen stir-fry
vegetables, thawed

12 oz pork cutlets or boneless
thin-cut pork chops, cut in strips

1 Tbsp cornstarch

GARNISH: sliced scallions

1. Bring 6 cups water to a boil on stovetop or in microwave. Add ramen noodles (reserve flavoring packets). Let stand 5 minutes or until tender; drain.

2. Meanwhile, heat 1 tsp of the oil in a large nonstick skillet. Add onion and cook, stirring often, 5 minutes or until tender. Add garlic; cook 1 minute or until fragrant.

3. Add vegetables; stir-fry 3 minutes or until crisp-tender. Remove to a bowl.

4. Heat remaining oil in same skillet. Add pork (in 2 batches if necessary). Stir-fry 2 minutes or until browned and cooked through. Remove to bowl with vegetables.

5. Stir 1 cup water, the seasoning packets and the cornstarch in skillet until blended; bring to a simmer, stirring. Cook 1 minute or until slightly thickened.

6. Add noodles; toss to coat. Add vegetables and pork; toss to mix and coat. Cook over low heat, tossing, until warmed through.

PER SERVING: **428 cal, 24 g pro, 42 g car, 3 g fiber, 17 g fat (6 g sat fat), 59 mg chol, 563 mg sod**

Veggie Fried Rice

COOKED MEAT · SKILLET · SERVES 4 · ACTIVE: 8 MIN · TOTAL: 15 MIN

✳️

2 tsp oil

1 bag (16 oz) frozen broccoli stir-fry blend

2 cups cooked chicken, ham, pork or beef, cut in strips

2 tsp minced garlic

2 cups cooked brown or white rice

2 large eggs, lightly beaten

3 Tbsp reduced-sodium soy sauce

2 Tbsp rice wine or cider vinegar

2 scallions, sliced (optional)

1. Heat oil in large nonstick skillet over high heat. Add frozen vegetables; stir-fry 2 minutes. Add chicken and garlic; cook 2 minutes more. Stir in rice; heat through.

2. Make a well in rice mixture or push it to one side of skillet; add eggs and stir-fry 1 minute. Remove from heat; stir in soy sauce and vinegar. Sprinkle with scallions, if desired. Serve with additional soy sauce.

PER SERVING: **351 cal, 28 g pro, 32 g car, 4 g fiber, 11 g fat (3 g sat fat), 168 mg chol, 522 mg sod**

Dijon-Crusted Pork Chops

PORK LOIN CHOPS • SKILLET & OVEN • SERVES 4 • ACTIVE: 15 MIN • TOTAL: 15 MIN

2 Tbsp Dijon mustard

¾ cup seasoned dried bread crumbs

4 pork loin chops, ¾ in. thick (about 1½ lb)

1 Tbsp canola oil

8 oz wide egg noodles

1¼ cups frozen mixed vegetables

1 Tbsp butter

¼ tsp each salt and pepper

1. Heat oven to 350°F. Place a sheet of foil on your kitchen counter. Measure mustard and bread crumbs separately onto foil. Coat pork chops with mustard, then coat with bread crumbs.

2. Heat oil in a large nonstick skillet over medium-high heat. Add chops and cook 2 to 3 minutes on each side, until bread crumbs are browned. Transfer to a foil-lined baking pan and bake 5 minutes or until cooked through.

3. Meanwhile, in a large saucepan, heat 4 quarts water to a rapid boil over high heat. Add noodles and cook according to package directions. Add vegetables in the last 5 minutes of cooking. Drain and toss with butter, salt and pepper; serve with pork chops.

PER SERVING: **577 cal, 33 g pro, 57 g car, 4 g fiber, 23 g fat (8 g sat fat), 108 mg chol, 795 mg sod**

68

Rosemary Chicken & Vegetables

CHICKEN DRUMSTICKS · OVEN · SERVES 4 · ACTIVE: 10 MIN · TOTAL: 40 MIN

❁

8 small chicken drumsticks
(about 1¾ lb)

4 large red potatoes, each
cut in 8 wedges, wedges halved

2 large peppers,
cut in ¾-in. wedges

1 large red onion,
cut in ½-in.-thick slices

2 Tbsp olive oil

3 Tbsp chopped fresh rosemary

2 Tbsp chopped garlic

½ tsp each salt and pepper

¼ cup pitted Kalamata olives,
cut in half

SERVE WITH: balsamic vinegar

1. Heat oven to 500°F. Position racks to divide oven in thirds. Line 2 rimmed baking sheets with nonstick foil.

2. Distribute drumsticks, potatoes, peppers and onion evenly between pans. Drizzle with oil; sprinkle with rosemary, garlic, salt and pepper. Toss to turn and coat.

3. Roast pans 15 minutes; remove from oven. Gently toss mixtures on pans, return to oven and roast 15 minutes longer, or until chicken is cooked through and vegetables are tender.

4. Arrange on serving platter; sprinkle with olives. Serve drizzled with vinegar. (To reduce fat and cholesterol, remove skin from chicken before eating.)

PER SERVING: **372 cal, 28 g pro, 35 g car, 5 g fiber, 14 g fat (3 g sat fat), 76 mg chol, 506 mg sod**

Barbecue Chicken

CHICKEN · GRILL · SERVES 4 · ACTIVE: 15 MIN ·
TOTAL: 40 MIN PLUS AT LEAST 1 HR MARINATING

✳

½ cup each chili sauce and molasses

2 tsp salt-free chili powder

1 tsp ground cumin

3½ lb chicken, cut in eighths

⅓ cup ginger ale

1. Mix chili sauce, molasses, chili powder and cumin in a large ziptop freezer bag. Add chicken, seal bag and refrigerate at least 1 hour or overnight.

2. Heat outdoor grill for indirect cooking. Remove chicken to foil-lined tray. Pour off marinade into a small glass bowl. Cook marinade in microwave on high 3 minutes, stirring often. Stir in ginger ale; set aside.

3. Place chicken, skin side up, on side of grill not directly over heat. Close grill; cook 30 minutes.

4. Place chicken, skin side down, directly over heat, brush with some marinade mixture and grill 5 minutes. Turn, brush with marinade and grill 5 minutes more.

PER SERVING: **528 cal, 49 g pro, 26 g car, 2 g fiber, 24 g fat (7 g sat fat), 154 mg chol, 457 mg sod**

TIP: Limited grill space? Cook chicken on a foil-lined pan in the oven for 50 minutes at 350°F.

Grilled Chicken Risotto

CHICKEN BREASTS • GRILL • SERVES 4 • ACTIVE: 10 MIN • TOTAL: 30 MIN

❋

1 box (5.5 oz) Creamy Parmesan Risotto (we used Lundberg)

2 medium zucchini, sliced lengthwise ½ in. thick

2 boneless, skinless chicken breasts (about 12 oz)

1 Tbsp oil

½ tsp pepper

¼ cup thawed frozen peas

1 medium tomato, diced

1. Cook risotto as package directs.

2. Meanwhile, heat stovetop grill pan. Brush zucchini and chicken with oil, then sprinkle with pepper.

3. Grill zucchini 7 to 9 minutes and chicken 10 to 12 minutes, turning once, until zucchini is tender and chicken is cooked through.

4. Remove chicken and zucchini to cutting board; cut into bite-size pieces.

5. When risotto is finished cooking, stir in peas, tomato, chicken and zucchini; remove from heat.

PER SERVING: **295 cal, 24 g pro, 33 g car, 3 g fiber, 8 g fat (2 g sat fat), 50 mg chol, 546 mg sod**

Chicken Enchiladas

COOKED CHICKEN • OVEN • SERVES 5 • ACTIVE: 15 MIN • TOTAL: 1 HR 5 MIN

❄

3 cups shredded cooked chicken

1 cup reduced-fat sour cream

1 cup cilantro, chopped

1 red bell pepper, chopped

1½ tsp minced garlic

1 tsp ground cumin

1 can (4.5 oz) chopped green chiles

1 cup (4 oz) shredded Monterey Jack cheese

1 jar (16 oz) green salsa

½ cup water

1 pkg (10 oz) flour tortillas

1. Grease a 13 x 9-in. baking dish.

2. In a bowl, mix chicken, ½ cup each of the sour cream and cilantro, the pepper, garlic, cumin, chiles and ¼ cup cheese.

3. Purée salsa, water, and remaining sour cream and cilantro in a blender or food processor. Spread 1 cup over bottom of prepared dish.

4. Spoon ⅓ cup chicken mixture down center of each tortilla. Roll up and place in baking dish. Bake and serve or cover and refrigerate, along with rest of sauce and cheese, up to 2 days.

5. To SERVE: Heat oven to 350°F. Pour remaining sauce over tortillas; bake uncovered 35 minutes. Sprinkle with remaining cheese and bake 15 minutes longer, or until bubbly.

PER SERVING: 562 cal, 39 g pro, 44 g car, 2 g fiber, 24 g fat (10 g sat fat), 115 mg chol, 964 mg sod

Cuban Chicken

CHICKEN DRUMSTICKS & THIGHS • SLOW COOKER • SERVES 4 •
ACTIVE: 10 MIN • TOTAL: 5 TO 8 HR ON LOW

1 medium onion, thinly sliced

4 tsp chopped garlic (4 cloves)

4 each chicken drumsticks and thighs, skin removed (about 4½ lb)

¼ cup each lime juice and orange juice

2 tsp ground cumin

½ tsp each paprika, salt and pepper

SERVE WITH: rice

GARNISH: Chopped cilantro (optional)

1. Place onion and garlic in a 6-qt slow cooker; arrange chicken on top.

2. Stir juices, cumin, paprika, salt and pepper in measuring cup; pour over chicken. Cook on low 5 to 8 hours until chicken is cooked through.

3. Serve chicken over rice; spoon juices with onions on top. Sprinkle with cilantro, if using.

PER SERVING: 211 cal, 30 g pro, 8 g car, 1 g fiber, 6 g fat (1 g sat fat), 116 mg chol, 420 mg sod

Creamy Chicken & Biscuits

CHICKEN THIGHS • OVEN • SERVES 6 • ACTIVE: 10 MIN • TOTAL: 40 MIN

1 tsp oil

12 oz boneless, skinless chicken thighs, fat trimmed, cut bite-size

1 cup baby carrots, halved lengthwise

8 oz sliced mushrooms

2 cans (10¾ oz each) condensed cream of chicken soup

1⅓ cups fat-free milk

1 Tbsp Dijon mustard

1 cup Heart Smart pancake and baking mix (Bisquick)

3 Tbsp chopped dill

⅓ cup frozen peas

3 scallions, sliced

1. Heat oven to 400°F. Heat oil in an 11- to 12-in. nonstick ovenproof skillet. Add chicken and cook over medium-high heat, stirring often, 3 minutes or until lightly browned.

2. Stir in carrots and mushrooms. Cover and cook 5 minutes, stirring occasionally, until mushrooms release some of their liquid and carrots are almost crisp-tender.

3. Stir in soup, 1 cup of the milk and the mustard until blended; bring to a simmer. Meanwhile, mix baking mix, 1 Tbsp of the dill and the remaining ⅓ cup milk in a small bowl until blended.

4. Stir remaining 2 Tbsp dill, the peas and scallions into skillet. Remove from heat and spoon 8 dollops (about 1 Tbsp each) biscuit dough on top.

5. Bake 15 to 20 minutes or until biscuits are golden and cooked through.

PER SERVING: **283 cal, 19 g pro, 29 g car, 2 g fiber, 10 g fat (2 g sat fat), 56 mg chol, 1,033 mg sod**

Fillo-Topped Moroccan Chicken

COOKED CHICKEN • SKILLET & OVEN • SERVES 7 • ACTIVE: 20 MIN • TOTAL: 45 MIN

※

1 cup slivered almonds

¼ cup confectioners' sugar, plus extra for sprinkling if desired

1½ tsp pumpkin pie spice

3 Tbsp butter

2 cups chopped onion

½ tsp each ground cumin and salt

2 cups shredded carrots

1½ cups chicken broth

5 cups shredded cooked chicken (1 rotisserie chicken)

½ cup raisins

⅓ cup chopped cilantro

6 fillo sheets, thawed

1. Heat oven to 400°F. Process almonds, confectioners' sugar and 1 tsp pumpkin pie spice 30 seconds until finely chopped.

2. Heat 1 Tbsp butter in a large skillet over medium heat. Add onion and cook 5 minutes until softened. Add remaining ½ tsp pumpkin pie spice, the cumin and salt; cook 1 minute. Stir in carrots and ¾ cup chicken broth; cook 1 minute or until carrots are softened. Remove from heat; stir in chicken, raisins and cilantro until well mixed.

3. Coat a 2-qt shallow baking dish with nonstick cooking spray; sprinkle ½ cup almond mixture over bottom. Spoon chicken mixture into casserole; sprinkle with remaining almond mixture. Evenly pour remaining chicken broth on top.

4. Melt remaining 2 Tbsp butter. Place one sheet of fillo on work surface at a time. Brush lightly with some melted butter. Using a pizza cutter, cut crosswise into strips (about ½ in. each). Place strips randomly on top of chicken mixture. Continue with remaining fillo and butter. Bake 20 to 25 minutes until filling is hot and fillo is browned. Sprinkle casserole with additional confectioners' sugar, if desired.

PER SERVING: 434 cal, 31 g pro, 33 g car, 4 g fiber, 20 g fat (6 g sat fat), 88 mg chol, 477 mg sod

Rigatoni Bolognese

TURKEY SAUSAGE · SKILLET · SERVES 6 · ACTIVE: 20 MIN · TOTAL: 35 MIN

1 box (1 lb) rigatoni pasta

2 medium carrots (4 oz), halved

1 medium onion (6 oz), quartered

1 pkg (8 or 10 oz) whole mushrooms

2 cloves garlic, peeled

2 tsp olive oil

3 links Italian turkey sausage (about 10 oz), casings removed

½ tsp crushed rosemary

¼ tsp each salt and pepper

½ cup white wine (optional)

1 can (28 oz) crushed tomatoes in thick purée

1. Cook pasta in a large pot of salted boiling water as box directs. Meanwhile, put carrots, onion, mushrooms and garlic in a food processor; pulse until finely chopped.

2. Heat oil in a large nonstick skillet over medium-high heat. Sauté chopped vegetables 6 minutes.

3. Add turkey sausage and cook, breaking up clumps, 4 minutes or until no longer pink. Stir in rosemary, salt, pepper and wine, if using; boil 1 minute.

4. Stir in crushed tomatoes, reduce heat and simmer, covered, 5 minutes. Spoon over drained pasta.

PER SERVING: 460 cal, 22 g pro, 75 g car, 5 g fiber, 8 g fat (2 g sat fat), 29 mg chol, 698 mg sod

Double Onion, Kielbasa & Potato Roast with Mustard Sauce

TURKEY KIELBASA • OVEN • SERVES 4 • ACTIVE: 15 MIN • TOTAL: 30 MIN

MUSTARD SAUCE

½ cup reduced-fat sour cream

2 Tbsp country-style Dijon mustard

1 Tbsp water

2 leeks, chopped

1 large sweet onion, cut into
½-in.-thick wedges

4 tsp oil

4 carrots, cut in 1½-in. pieces

5 medium Yukon gold potatoes,
cut lengthwise in quarters, then
halved crosswise

¼ tsp each salt and pepper

1 turkey or beef kielbasa (14 oz),
cut in 2-in. pieces, then halved
lengthwise

1. Position racks to divide oven in thirds. Heat oven to 500°F. Line 2 rimmed baking pans with nonstick foil.

2. MUSTARD SAUCE: Combine sauce ingredients; chill.

3. Toss leeks and onion with 2 tsp of the oil on one baking pan. Toss carrots and potatoes on other pan with remaining 2 tsp oil. Sprinkle all with salt and pepper.

4. Place leeks and onions on top rack, carrots and potatoes on bottom. Roast 15 minutes.

5. Remove pans from oven; toss. Add kielbasa to carrots and potatoes. Return to oven; roast 15 minutes more until vegetables are tender. Toss kielbasa with vegetables; pass the mustard sauce.

PER SERVING: **484 cal, 18 g pro, 45 g car, 5 g fiber, 26 g fat (9 g sat fat), 81 mg chol, 1,593 mg sod**

Spaghetti & Meatballs

GROUND TURKEY • OVEN • SERVES 6 • ACTIVE: 25 MIN • TOTAL: 1 HR

½ cup bulgur

1 lb ground turkey

2 Tbsp each grated Parmesan and chopped parsley

2 cloves garlic, minced

1 Tbsp dried minced onion flakes

1 large egg white

½ tsp Italian seasoning

¼ tsp pepper

1 box (13.25 oz) whole-grain spaghetti

1 jar (24 to 26 oz) marinara sauce

1. Put bulgur in medium bowl. Add boiling water to cover; let soak 15 minutes. Drain well; return to bowl.

2. Heat oven to 425°F. Line a rimmed baking sheet with nonstick foil. Add turkey, Parmesan, parsley, garlic, onion flakes, egg white, Italian seasoning and pepper to bulgur. Mix lightly with a fork until blended.

3. Form mixture into 18 meatballs (1 slightly rounded Tbsp each) and place on baking sheet. Bake 15 minutes or until lightly browned.

4. Meanwhile, cook pasta in large pot of salted boiling water as box directs. Warm marinara sauce in medium saucepan; add meatballs. Drain pasta and serve with meatballs and sauce.

PER SERVING: 475 cal, 32 g pro, 73 g car, 11 g fiber, 6 g fat (1 g sat fat), 51 mg chol, 686 mg sod

Cioppino

2 cups thinly sliced fennel

2 leeks (white and pale green parts only), rinsed and thinly sliced (1 cup)

12 oz small red potatoes, quartered

1 jar (26 oz) marinara sauce

1 can (14½ oz) chicken broth

1 cup water

⅓ cup dry red wine (optional)

1 tsp fennel seeds (optional)

¼ tsp hot pepper flakes

24 cleaned mussels

12 sea scallops, halved if very large

1 lb skinless halibut fillet, cut into 1½-in. chunks

SERVE WITH: sourdough bread and olive oil for drizzling

1. Mix all ingredients except seafood in a 5-qt or larger slow cooker.

2. Cover and cook on low 7 to 9 hours until vegetables are tender.

3. Raise heat to high; stir in seafood. Cover and cook 20 to 40 minutes until mussels open and seafood is cooked.

PER SERVING: **297 cal, 33 g pro,
28 g car, 4 g fiber, 6 g fat (1 g sat fat),
54 mg chol, 943 mg sod**

Jambalaya

TURKEY KIELBASA & SHRIMP • SLOW COOKER • SERVES 5 •
ACTIVE: 10 MIN • TOTAL: 4½ TO 5½ HR ON LOW

1 medium red onion, finely chopped

1 green bell pepper, chopped

2 ribs celery, thinly sliced

8 oz turkey kielbasa, sliced

1 can (28 oz) whole tomatoes

1 cup uncooked converted rice

2 tsp salt-free Cajun-Creole seasoning (we used The Spice Hunter)

12 oz peeled large shrimp (21 to 25 count)

GARNISH: chopped parsley and hot pepper sauce

1. Layer onion, pepper, celery and turkey kielbasa in a 3½-qt or larger slow cooker.

2. Mix tomatoes and their juices, rice and seasoning in medium bowl, breaking up tomatoes with a spoon. Pour in slow cooker. Cover and cook on low 4 to 5 hours until vegetables and rice are tender.

3. Stir in shrimp, cover and cook 20 minutes until cooked through. Sprinkle with parsley and hot sauce.

PER SERVING: **325 cal, 26 g pro, 44 g car, 3 g fiber, 5 g fat (1 g sat fat), 133 mg chol, 744 mg sod**

Grilled Vegetable Lasagna

VEGETARIAN • GRILL & OVEN • SERVES 9 • ACTIVE: 30 MIN • TOTAL: 1 HR 15 MIN

1 package (8 oz) oven-ready lasagna noodles

3 small zucchini (1 lb), sliced lengthwise ½ in. thick

1 small eggplant (12 oz), sliced lengthwise ½ in. thick

2 yellow peppers, quartered, seeded

Nonstick cooking spray

1 container (15 oz) fat-free ricotta

4 oz fat-free cream cheese, softened

1 jar (24 to 26 oz) marinara sauce

1¼ cups shredded reduced-fat mozzarella

2 Tbsp grated Parmesan

GARNISH: chopped parsley

1. Heat outdoor grill or stovetop grill pan.

2. Put noodles and water to cover in a 13 x 9-in. baking dish. Let soak 15 minutes or until slightly softened and pliable.

3. Meanwhile, coat vegetables with cooking spray. Grill 8 to 12 minutes, turning as needed, until lightly charred and tender. Remove to a cutting board and cut into bite-size pieces. Toss to mix.

4. Heat oven to 375°F. Remove noodles to paper towels. Drain water from baking dish and wipe dry. Mix ricotta, cream cheese and 2 Tbsp water in a bowl until well blended.

5. Spread ½ cup marinara sauce in bottom of baking dish. Lay 3 noodles crosswise on top. Spread noodles with ⅔ cup ricotta mixture. Top with 1 cup vegetables, ⅔ cup sauce, ¼ cup mozzarella and 2 tsp Parmesan. Repeat layers twice.

6. Top with remaining noodles and sauce (set aside the remaining vegetables and mozzarella). Cover with foil and bake 30 minutes.

7. Uncover, top with remaining vegetables and cheese, and bake 15 minutes or until noodles are tender when pierced in center and cheese is melted.

PER SERVING: **276 cal, 18 g pro, 38 g car, 5 g fiber, 6 g fat (2 g sat fat), 16 mg chol, 594 mg sod**

Perfect Potato Salad

VEGETARIAN • STOVETOP • SERVES 8 • ACTIVE: 15 MIN • TOTAL: 2½ HR

2½ lb red-skinned potatoes, cut into 1-in. chunks

1 cup fresh corn kernels

3 Tbsp cider vinegar

½ tsp salt

¼ tsp pepper

½ cup each light mayonnaise and plain fat-free yogurt

⅓ cup water

1 tsp Dijon mustard

¾ cup each chopped celery and sliced scallions

½ cup chopped fresh dill

1. Bring potatoes and enough water to cover to a boil. Reduce heat and simmer 6 minutes or until potatoes are almost tender.

2. Add corn; simmer 1 minute or until potatoes are tender and corn crisp-tender. Drain. Transfer to bowl and toss with vinegar, salt and pepper. Cool.

3. In another bowl, stir mayonnaise, yogurt, water and mustard until smooth. Add potato mixture, celery, scallions and dill; toss to mix and coat thoroughly. Cover and refrigerate at least 2 hours.

TIP: This salad tastes better made the day before serving so the flavors get to blend together.

PER SERVING: 179 cal, 4 g pro, 30 g car, 3 g fiber, 5 g fat (1 g sat fat), 6 mg chol, 309 mg sod

Vegetable Curry

1 can (14 oz) light coconut milk

¼ cup all-purpose flour

1½ Tbsp red curry paste

1 large onion, chopped

4 small Yukon gold potatoes (8 oz), halved

4 cups 1½-in. chunks butternut squash

4 cups cauliflower florets

1 can (15 oz) chickpeas, rinsed

1 red bell pepper, cut in 1-in. pieces

1 cup frozen peas

3 cups cooked basmati rice

GARNISH: chopped cilantro

1. Whisk coconut milk, flour and curry paste in a 3½-qt or larger slow cooker. Stir in vegetables except peas; mix well.

2. Cover and cook on low 6 to 7 hours until vegetables are tender. Stir in peas, cover and let sit 5 minutes. Serve with rice; garnish with cilantro.

PER SERVING: **355 cal, 11 g pro, 63 g car, 10 g fiber, 7 g fat (3 g sat fat), 0 mg chol, 244 mg sod**

Curried Cauliflower Soup

VEGETABLES • STOVETOP • MAKES 10 CUPS • ACTIVE: 10 MIN • TOTAL: 30 MIN

❉

2 tsp oil

1 large onion, chopped

2 medium carrots, sliced
¼ in. thick

2 Tbsp curry powder

2 cloves garlic, minced

2 cans (14.5 oz each) chicken broth,
or 3½ cups broth or bouillon

2½ cups water

2 medium potatoes (8 oz),
cut in ½-in. pieces

3 cups frozen cauliflower florets

1 can (15.5 oz) chickpeas, rinsed

½ cup frozen cut-leaf spinach

SERVE WITH: plain yogurt

1. Heat oil in large saucepan over medium-high heat. Add onions and carrots; cook 4 minutes or until onions are golden and just tender.

2. Stir in curry powder and garlic; cook 30 seconds or until fragrant. Stir in remaining ingredients; cook, covered, 15 minutes or until vegetables are tender.

PER 1-CUP SERVING: **110 cal, 4 g pro, 20 g car, 5 g fiber, 2 g fat (0 g sat fat), 0 mg chol, 272 mg sod**

Spinach-Rice Cakes

VEGETARIAN • SKILLET & OVEN • SERVES 4 • ACTIVE: 10 MIN • TOTAL: 50 MIN

❀

2 tsp oil

½ cup chopped onion

2 cloves garlic, minced

1 box (10 oz) frozen leaf spinach, thawed and coarsely cut

2¼ cups water

1 cup long-grain rice

½ cup grated Parmesan

¼ tsp pepper

1 large egg

2 oz part-skim mozzarella, shredded

2 cups marinara sauce

1. Heat oil in a large nonstick skillet over high heat. Sauté onion and garlic 2 minutes. Add spinach and water; bring to a boil.

2. Stir in rice; cover and simmer 20 minutes or until water is absorbed. Heat oven to 350°F. Line a large baking sheet with nonstick foil.

3. Transfer rice to bowl; stir in Parmesan and pepper. Mix in egg. For each cake, scoop and flatten ¼ cup rice mixture onto baking sheet.

4. Bake 20 minutes or until firm. Sprinkle tops with mozzarella; return to oven 1 minute to melt. Serve with warmed marinara.

PER SERVING: **562 cal, 25 g pro, 66 g car, 6 g fiber, 22 g fat (8 g sat fat), 100 mg chol, 1,406 mg sod**

Photo Credits

Available in the same series:

Monday Night is Chicken Night
Tuesday Night is Pasta Night
Wednesday Night is Vegetarian
Thursday Night is Hearty Meat
Friday Night is Seafood Night

Copyright © 2010 Hachette
Filipacchi Media U.S., Inc.

First published in 2010 in the
United States of America by
Filipacchi Publishing
1633 Broadway
New York, NY 10019

Woman's Day is a registered
trademark of Hachette Filipacchi
Media U.S., Inc.

Design: Patricia Fabricant
Editor: Lauren Kuczala
Manufacturing: Lynn Scaglione
and Annie Andres

ISBN-13: 978-1-936297-01-6

Library of Congress Control
Number: 2010921563

Printed in China

Page 2: Mary Ellen Bartley; p. 6: Amy Kalyn Sims; p. 8: Mary Ellen Bartley; pp. 9, 11, 12, 13: Amy Kalyn Sims; p. 14: Mary Ellen Bartley; pp. 15, 17: Anastassios Mentis; p. 18: Kate Sears; p. 19: Ann Stratton; p. 20: Mary Ellen Bartley; p. 21: Steve Giralt; p. 22: Mary Ellen Bartley; p. 24: Ann Stratton; pp. 25, 27: Mary Ellen Bartley; pp. 28, 29, 30, 31: Kate Sears; p. 32: Tom McWilliam; p. 33: Jim Franco; p. 34: Iain Bagwell; p. 35: John Blais; p. 37: Jonny Valiant; p. 38: Ann Stratton; pp. 39, 40: Mary Ellen Bartley; p. 43: Iain Bagwell; p. 44: Mary Ellen Bartley; p. 46: Mark Thomas; pp. 47, 48: Mary Ellen Bartley; p. 52: Jonny Valiant; p. 55: Mary Ellen Bartley; p. 56: Mark Thomas; p. 57: Shaffer Smith; pp. 59, 60: Mary Ellen Bartley; p. 63: Amy Kalyn Sims; p. 64: Con Poulos; p. 67: Iain Bagwell; p. 68: Mary Ellen Bartley; p. 69: Ann Stratton; p. 71: Mary Ellen Bartley; p. 72: Jim Franco; p. 74: Mark Thomas; p. 75: Mary Ellen Bartley; pp. 76, 79: Alison Miksch; p. 81: Jim Franco; p. 82: Jonny Valiant; p. 84: Jim Franco; pp. 86, 87: Kate Sears; p. 89: Jim Franco; p. 90: Mary Ellen Bartley; p. 91: Kate Sears; p. 93: Iain Bagwell; p. 94: Con Poulos.